How to Dazzle at
Reading

Irene Yates

Brilliant
PUBLICATIONS

We hope you and your class enjoy using this book. Other books in the series include:

English Titles
How to Dazzle at Grammar   978 1 897675 46 5
How to Dazzle at Writing   978 1 897675 45 8
How to Dazzle at Reading for Meaning   978 1 897675 51 9
How to Dazzle at Spelling   978 1 897675 47 2
How to Dazzle at Macbeth   978 1 897675 93 9
How to Dazzle at Twelfth Night   978 1 903853 34 4
How to Dazzle at Romeo and Juliet   978 1 897675 92 2

Maths Titles
How to Dazzle at Oral and Mental Starters   978 1 903853 10 8
How to Dazzle at Algebra   978 1 903853 12 2
How to Dazzle at Written Calculations   978 1 903853 11 5
How to Dazzle at Maths Crosswords (Book 1)   978 1 903853 38 2
How to Dazzle at Maths Crosswords (Book 2)   978 1 903853 39 9

Science Titles
How to Dazzle at Being a Scientist   978 1 897675 52 6
How to Dazzle at Scientific Enquiry   978 1 903853 15 3

Other Titles
How to Dazzle at Beginning Mapskills   978 1 903853 58 0
How to Dazzle at Information Technology   978 1 897675 67 0

To find out more details on any of our resources, please log onto our website: www.brilliantpublications.co.uk.

Published by Brilliant Publications,
Unit 10, Sparrow Hall Farm,
Edlesborough, Dunstable, Bedfordshire LU6 2ES

email: info@brilliantpublications.co.uk
website: www.brilliantpublications.co.uk

General enquiries
Tel: 01525 222292

The name Brilliant Publications and its logo are registered trademarks.

Written by Irene Yates
Illustrated by Darin Mount

© Irene Yates 1998
Printed ISBN: 978 1 897675 44 1
ebook ISBN: 978 0 85747 085 0

First published 1998. Reprinted 1999, 2009 and 2012.
Printed in the UK
10 9 8 7 6 5 4

Contents

Introduction

How to Dazzle at Reading contains 42 photocopiable sheets for use with Key Stage 3 pupils who are working at levels 1-3 of the National Curriculum in English (Scottish levels A-B). The activities are presented in an adolescent-friendly manner and provide a flexible but structured resource for teaching pupils:
- to understand and use decoding techniques
- to discriminate between different sounds in words
- to learn letters and letter combinations
- to read words by sounding out and blending the sounds.

Because there is so much to remember, it is difficult for pupils with special needs to assimilate all they need to know to make their decoding fluent. Most letter combinations and blends require reinforcement many times before they are understood. It is only when those concepts are understood that they become part of the pupils' own communication abilities. Many pupils of this age, working at levels 1-3, need to be working at word and sentence level far more frequently than at text level.

The small steps covered in the activities in this book will help pupils to develop their visual and aural skills of discrimination, recognition and memory. Many of the strategies can be modified and adapted to suit the specific needs of your pupils. It is not possible within the confines of this book to tackle every single phoneme or grapheme that the pupil may find difficult, so the sheets focus on those which are most commonly confusing to pupils of this age, working at this level.

Part of the disaffection of pupils with special needs is the misery of failing time after time. The sheets are designed, with information and questioning, to help those pupils to experience success and achievement. The expectation that the pupil *will* achieve will help to build confidence and competence.

The tasks in this book are kept fairly short, to facilitate concentration. The text on the pages is kept to a minimum, and the content of the pages is applied to contexts that the pupils will find motivating. In many cases there is an element of puzzle or competition to the activities to provide greater motivation. The extra task at the bottom of each sheet provides reinforcement and enables pupils to use the skills they have learned in a functional way.

How to use the book

The activity pages are designed to supplement any English language activities you pursue in the classroom. They are intended to add to your pupils' knowledge of how the English language works.

They can be used with individual pupils, pairs or very small groups, as the need arises. The text on the pages has been kept as short as possible, so that reluctant or poorer readers will not feel swamped by 'words on the page'. For the same reason, we have used white space and boxes, to help the pupils to understand the sheets easily, and to give them a measure of independence in working through them. In many instances, a pair of scissors and encouragement to 'cut and paste' will further help the pupils to work through the sheets.

It is not the author's intention that a teacher should expect all the pupils to complete all the sheets, rather that the sheets be used with a flexible approach, so that the book provides a bank of resources that will meet needs as they arise.

Many of the sheets can be modified and extended in very simple ways. The Add-ons can provide a good vehicle for discussion of what has been learned and how it can be applied.

The companion book to this one is *How to Dazzle at Reading for Meaning*, which concentrates, as the title suggests, on understanding rather than decoding. Together the two books can provide a balance which will help your pupils to gain fluency and confidence.

Circle the letter

Draw a ring round the sound you hear at the beginning of each word.

Write the words underneath each picture.

Add-on
Choose one word. Write three sentences about it.

How to Dazzle at Reading
www.brilliantpublications.co.uk

Match the beginning sounds

Draw a line from the pictures to the letter that begins their name.

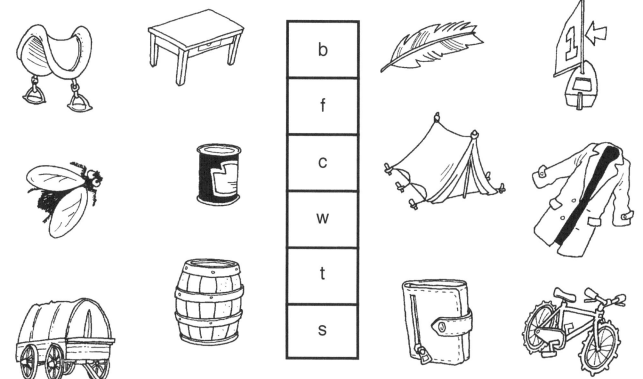

Write the words here:

b _____   w _____

b _____   w _____

f _____   t _____

f _____   t _____

c _____   s _____

c _____   s _____

Add-on
Use a dictionary to check your spellings.

Begins with bl, br, cl, cr, dr or dw

Look at the words below. Read them carefully. Write them in the column where they belong.

Time yourself.

brag	cloud	crag	dwell	black
cress	clap	drive	dwarf	block
dweller	broad	creep	brow	bloom
climb	drink	clever	dry	dwelling
cricket	dwindle	bleak	dream	

bl __	br __	cl __	cr __	dr __	dw __

It took me _____ minutes to work out these lists.

Add-on
Find three more words beginning with these sounds: bl, br and dr.
Use a dictionary.

Begins with fl, fr, gl, gr, pl or pr

Look at the words below. Read them carefully. Write them in the column where they belong.

Time yourself.

flag	glum	fry	plucky	flabby
friend	glory	pretend	Friday	flat
prawn	front	present	grab	glad
press	great	plum	please	granny
flea	grapple	glance	plot	

fl __	fr __	gl __	gr __	pl __	pr __

It took me _____ minutes to work out these lists.

Add-on
Find another three words for each list.
Use a dictionary.

Begins with sc, scr, sk, sl, sm or sn

Look at the words below. Read them carefully. Write them in the column where they belong.

Time yourself.

scallywag	skate	scribble	sniff	scrum
scale	smart	scare	sleet	snooze
slink	screen	smell	skim	scrimp
snug	smug	sky	smooth	sleep
snip	sketch	slip		

sc ___	scr ___	sk ___	sl ___	sm ___	sn ___

It took me _____ minutes to work out these lists.

Add-on
Find another three words for each list.
Use a dictionary.

Begins with sp, spl, spr, squ, st or str

Look at the words below. Read them carefully. Write them in the column where they belong.

Time yourself.

spaghetti	stream	split	square	splatter
spring	spanner	stick	spray	step
splutter	squeamish	sparkle	state	sprig
strong	splendid	splinter	squall	squeak
starve	stress	strap	spin	

sp __	spl __	spr __	squ __	st __	str __

It took me _____ minutes to work out these lists.

Add-on
Find another three words for each list.
Use a dictionary.

Begins with shr, sw, thr or tr

Look at the words below. Read them carefully. Write them in the column where they belong.

Time yourself.

thread	train	shrug	three	swallow
thrill	swish	throne	trail	shriek
swan	shrink	sweat	shrimp	shrill
swim	tramp	swing	tremble	trek
shred	through	throat	trick	

shr __	sw __	thr __	tr __

It took me _____ minutes to work out these lists.

Add-on
Find another three words for each list.
Use a dictionary.

Finish the words

Complete each of these words with one of these letter sounds:

d   s   t   r

One word won't fit. The word that doesn't fit is: [   ]

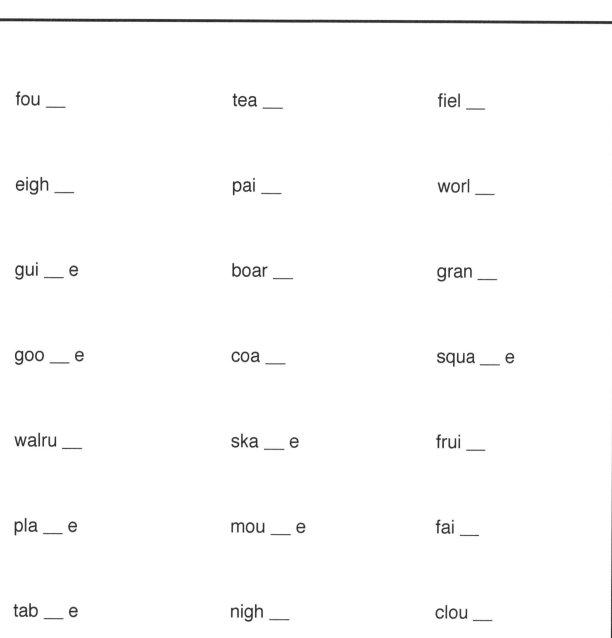

fou __   tea __   fiel __

eigh __   pai __   worl __

gui __ e   boar __   gran __

goo __ e   coa __   squa __ e

walru __   ska __ e   frui __

pla __ e   mou __ e   fai __

tab __ e   nigh __   clou __

Add-on
Choose six words and write a sentence for each one.

End sounds

Draw a ring round the sound that ends each picture name.

Write the words underneath each picture.

Add-on
Find six words that end with the sound 'n'.

Match the end sounds

Draw a line to match the pictures with the sound that ends their name.

p
t
k
g
r
n

Write the words here:

Add-on
Use a dictionary to check your spellings.

The vowels

Five letters of the alphabet are called vowels. They are:

a   e   i   o   u

All the words in this puzzle all use short vowel sounds.

Finish the puzzle.

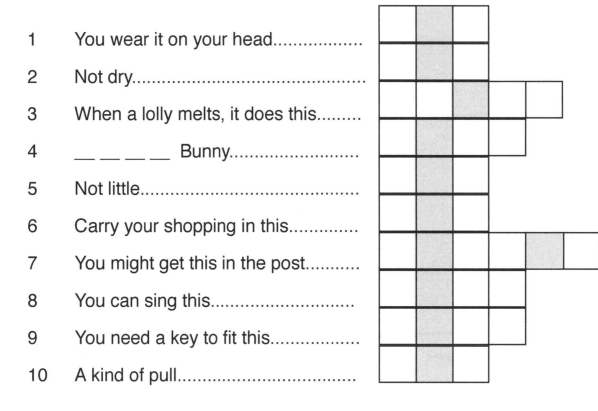

1   You wear it on your head..................

2   Not dry...

3   When a lolly melts, it does this.........

4   __ __ __ __ Bunny.........................

5   Not little...

6   Carry your shopping in this..............

7   You might get this in the post...........

8   You can sing this..............................

9   You need a key to fit this..................

10   A kind of pull....................................

Helpline
The vowels fit in the shaded boxes.

Add-on
Find ten more words with short vowels.

Short vowels

These letters are vowels. You can hear their sounds in different words.

a e i o u

Put the short vowel sounds into these words. Read the words, and say them out loud.

a	e	i	o	u
b __ ng	s __ nt	p __ ng	g __ t	b __ g
r __ ng	d __ nt	s __ ng	n __ t	m __ d
s __ ng	t __ nt	cl __ ng	fr __ g	cr __ mb
p __ nt	l __ nt	dr __ nk	l __ g	d __ mb
r __ nt	b __ nt	br __ nk	s __ ng	cl __ b
cl __ ng	b __ nd	th __ nk	pr __ ng	br __ sh
dr __ nk	t __ nd	l __ nk	ch __ p	n __ mb

Add-on
Think of two more words for each list
and write them down.

Long vowels

Sometimes vowels don't have the short vowel sounds which they have in 'bag', 'beg', 'big', 'bog' and 'bug'. When the vowel makes a different sound it is called a **long vowel sound**.

Find a long vowel word to rhyme with each of these words. The first one has been done for you.

Helpline
Watch out! The sound may not always be spelled in exactly the same way.

cage

page

train

name

feet

meet

seat

bite

high

kite

moon

grow

slope

tune

tube

blue

Add-on
Use your reading book to find ten more words
with long vowel sounds.

Two 'oo's

A short 'oo' says 'oo' as in b**oo**k.

A long 'oo' says 'oo' as in m**oo**n.

Write these words in the correct list.

room	spook	took	cook	loose
goose	tooth	shook	boom	good
foot	loom	broom	soon	boot
brook	hoof	spoon	crook	mood
nook	food	hook	rook	doom
gloom	school	drool	hood	cool

Short 'oo'	Long 'oo'

Add-on
Can you find any more words with two 'oo's
in the dictionary?

'oi' puzzle

In most words 'oi' sounds like 'oy' as in **toy**.

**All the words in this puzzle have 'oi' in them.
Can you complete the puzzle?**

1   You grow things in this...................................

2   When you can choose, you have this............

3   To raise (a flag) ....

3   A knee is one of these.............................

4   Don't drink this!.....................................

5   A pet with a shell...................................

7   Stick something together.........................

8   Damp..

9   Money...

10   A quiet corridor in an abbey.....................

11   Paper thin metal, for cooking....................

12   Do this to the water in the kettle.............

13   Hitting a drum hard is this.......................

14   Stick your finger at something ....

Add-on
Use your dictionary to find six more 'oi' words.

Rhyming words

Find three words to rhyme with each of these words.

Time yourself.

fly	_____	_____	_____
chick	_____	_____	_____
same	_____	_____	_____
bike	_____	_____	_____
cry	_____	_____	_____
phone	_____	_____	_____
clue	_____	_____	_____
away	_____	_____	_____
are	_____	_____	_____
fur	_____	_____	_____
bear	_____	_____	_____
bee	_____	_____	_____

It took me _____ minutes to finish this sheet.

Add-on
Use six of your words to write a poem.

Rhyming riddles

Find the missing word. It begins with the letter 't' and rhymes with the word in the box.

1   In these games everybody works together. _____ | seam |

2   You watch the clock for this. _____ | rhyme |

3   Some people have lots of this. _____ | waste |

4   Not short. _____ | wall |

5   Chatterboxes like to do this. _____ | walk |

6   Bullies often do this to other people. _____ | please |

Find three more words to rhyme with each of these words. Use any letter to begin.

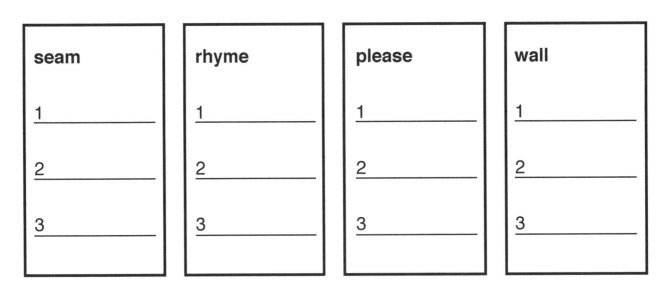

seam	rhyme	please	wall
1 _____	1 _____	1 _____	1 _____
2 _____	2 _____	2 _____	2 _____
3 _____	3 _____	3 _____	3 _____

Add-on
Think of six more words beginning with 't' and find three words to rhyme with each one.

Rhyming sense

Find the missing word. It begins with the letter 's' and rhymes with the word in the box.

1   When you get to the end you do this. _____ | drop |

2   This person is paid to find out secrets. _____ | dry |

3   Being good at this keeps you fit and healthy. _____ | short |

4   You can do this with glue. _____ | pick |

5   A loud screeching noise. _____ | peel |

6   How big or how small something is. _____ | prize |

Find three more words to rhyme with each of these words. Use any letter to begin.

pick	dry	peel	drop
1 _____	1 _____	1 _____	1 _____
2 _____	2 _____	2 _____	2 _____
3 _____	3 _____	3 _____	3 _____

Add-on
Think of six more words beginning with 's' and find three words to rhyme with each one.

What's this?

Choose the right word:

This is a _____. bike book boot	This is a _____. neck net neat	This is a _____. skirt scarf skate
This is a _____. kettle key knee	This is a _____. squib square squaw	This is a _____. towel trowel tower
This is a _____. yawn yacht yard	This is a _____. weed web well	This is a _____. cloak clod clock

Add-on
Choose one set of three words and write a sentence for each.

Which word?

Look at the pictures. Read the words. Draw lines to match the words to the pictures. You will have one word left over.

dog

mouse

spider

tree

muffin

space

apple

bike

football

The word left over is:

Add-on
Write three sentences about the word that is left over.

Which words match?

Read the words carefully. Draw rings round the words that match in each line.

One line has no words that match. Draw a line underneath it.

went	was	when	went	where
mum	my	make	many	mother
come	call	came	come	could
did	dog	does	does	don't
away	about	after	away	across
this	the	then	them	this
going	got	goes	going	great
night	next	new	now	new
other	once	out	other	over
first	father	found	first	follow
it	if	in	inside	if
those	thought	through	thought	thank

Add-on
Choose the line with no matching words and write a sentence for each word. Can you do it in less than ten minutes?

Matching the words

Read the words carefully. Draw rings round the words that match in each line.

One line has no words that match. Draw a line underneath it.

above	across	almost	across	along
light	leave	lady	little	leave
such	suddenly	sure	such	still
might	mother	morning	much	mother
paper	place	push	pull	put
want	water	way	water	why
year	young	your	year	you
both	bought	brought	bought	bother
eyes	every	earth	every	easy
their	there	them	their	these
dig	don't	down	door	down
girl	gone	great	garden	girl

Add-on
Choose the line with no matching words and write one sentence
for each word. Can you do it in less than ten minutes?

Learn the words

Read the words carefully. Each line has an odd word. Write it carefully and practise spelling it.

One line does not have an odd word. Draw a line underneath it.

always	about	about	about	_____
again	again	almost	again	_____
be	be	be	began	_____
down	down	don't	down	_____
here	head	here	here	_____
one	one	once	one	_____
put	put	place	put	_____
round	ran	ran	ran	_____
some	some	some	some	_____
that	those	that	that	_____
us	us	used	us	_____
who	whole	who	who	_____

Add-on
Choose three 'odd' words and write a sentence using each one.
Can you do it in less than five minutes?

Odd one out

Read the words carefully. Draw a ring round the word which is the odd one out in each line.

One line has not got an odd word. Draw a line underneath it.

too	too	too	took	too
tree	tree	trees	tree	tree
name	main	name	name	name
pull	pull	up	pull	pull
some	same	same	same	same
took	took	take	took	took
can't	came	can't	can't	can't
saw	saw	saw	was	saw
than	then	than	than	than
that	that	that	that	that
next	extra	next	next	next
little	small	little	little	little

Add-on
Choose three words and write a sentence for each one.
Can you do it in less than five minutes?

More odds

Read the words carefully. Draw a ring round the word which is the odd one out in each line.

One line has not got an odd word. Draw a line underneath it.

much	much	mulch	much	much
who	who	how	who	who
would	would	would	wood	would
should	show	should	should	should
could	could	could	cloud	could
school	school	scowl	school	school
these	this	these	these	these
tree	tree	tree	tree	three
again	again	again	again	again
jump	just	just	just	just
laugh	laugh	last	laugh	laugh
night	night	night	high	night

Add-on
Choose three words and write one sentence for each one.
Can you do it in less than five minutes?

Which fits?

Fit one of these words into each space in the story.

round   in   on   over   up

under   for   at   of   to

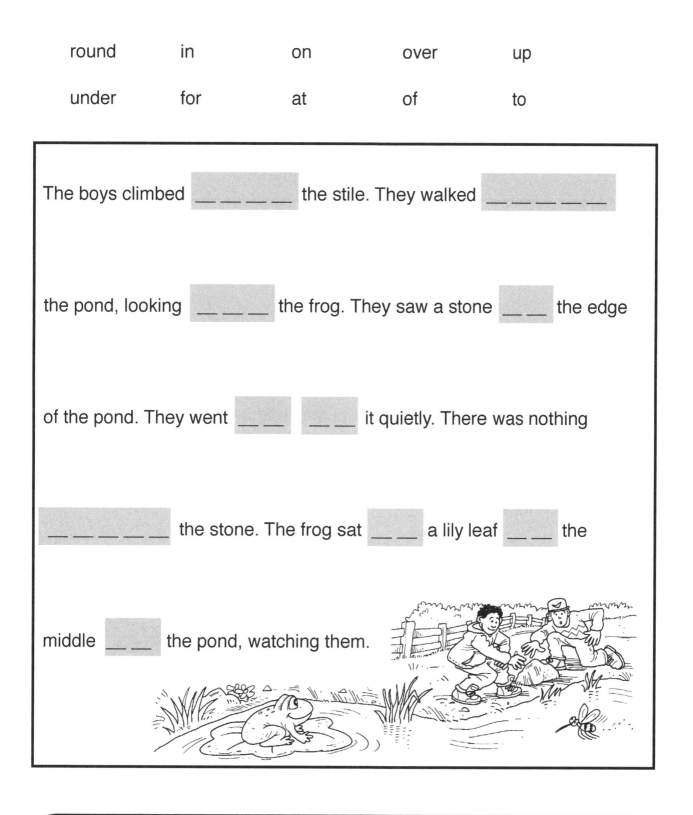

The boys climbed _ _ _ _ the stile. They walked _ _ _ _ _ _

the pond, looking _ _ _ the frog. They saw a stone _ _ _ the edge

of the pond. They went _ _ _ _ it quietly. There was nothing

_ _ _ _ _ _ the stone. The frog sat _ _ _ a lily leaf _ _ _ the

middle _ _ the pond, watching them.

Add-on
Write three more sentences to finish this story.

Eight 'm' words

Read these words carefully.

made	music	must
make	many	much
more	may	

Fit each word into one of these sentences:

They thought the dance would be a good way to _____ money.

The band said they wouldn't charge _____.

James _____ the tickets.

The _____ was brilliant!

So _____ people turned up, they had a wonderful time.

There _____ have been over a hundred people there!

They couldn't let any _____ in.

The dance was so successful, they _____ do it again!

Add-on
Write down six more words beginning with 'm' that are used a lot.
Write a sentence for each one.

Eight 'w' words

Read the words carefully.

with	water	were	when
what	would	went	wanted

Fit each word into one of these sentences:

Pete _____ swimming twice a week.

Pete and Joe _____ great friends.

Joe decided to go to the pool _____ Pete.

Joe could not swim _____ they first started going together.

Joe really _____ to learn to swim.

Pete thought Joe needed to feel safe in the _____.

Pete showed Joe _____ to do.

He _____ soon learn to swim.

Add-on
Write down six more 'w' words that are used a lot.
Write a sentence for each one.

Eight 'h' words

Read these words carefully.

had	half	help	him
his	home	house	how

Fit each word into one of these sentences:

Chris _____ an idea.

He thought he could build a tree _____.

Chris needed some _____.

Perhaps Gary would help _____.

Gary could see _____ they would do it.

Chris brought some wood from _____.

Gary got some rope from _____ dad's shed.

The tree house was _____ built when the neighbour shouted

at them.

Add-on
Write down six more 'h' words that are used a lot.
Write a sentence for each one.

Fill in the story

Read these words carefully.

They	fishing	the	for	first
sat	ages	got	the	bite
plenty	They	river	to	went
saw	of			

Fit the missing words into these sentences.

In the summer, Jack _____ _____

with his grandad. They went down _____ _____

_____. They had _____ _____ live bait.

_____ _____ _____

_____, waiting for the first bite. Grandad _____

_____ _____ _____ ,

then Jack. _____ _____ a kingfisher.

Add-on
Write three more sentences for this story.

What makes sense?

Write the word which makes the most sense in each space.

A praying mantis is a king/kind/link _____ of stick insect.

It gets its name from the way it holds/hears/horn _____

its large front legs. It looks as if it is praying. Really it is waiting to

crash/teach/catch _____ insects. As soon as the

insect gets close/clear/cloud _____ enough, the legs of

the praying mantis shout/shoot/touch _____ out to catch it.

The praying mantis hides itself on leaves the same colour as its body so

it is hard to set/sea/see _____ .

Add-on
Find out more about stick insects from a reference book.

How to Dazzle at Reading
www.brilliantpublications.co.uk

Choose the right word

Write the word which makes most sense in each space.

Sea horses are a kind of fish/fight/flash [ ].

They live in warm seas amongst the stranger/seaweed/sandwich

[ ]. They cling to seaweed with their

trim/teas/tails [ ]. Sea horses have heads shaped like

those of horses/houses/shores [ ]. They eat tiny shellfish

and other sea crocodile/creatures/crest [ ].

They suck their food through their narrow mouth at the

trip/tip/treat [ ] of a long tube-like snout.

Add-on
Find out about other strange sea-creatures
from a reference book.

Which word is right?

Write the word which makes most sense in each space.

Porcupines are covered in quills. The quills are long and

sharp/shape/shred [   ] . When a porcupine is

angry/angel/angle [   ] , it puffs up its

quilt/quills/quick [   ] and shakes them.

It stint/stamps/story [   ] its feet on the ground

to frighten its enemy. Then it turns round/race/rock [   ]

and chases the enemy. Porcupines sleep in the daytime and at night they

search for food/form/food [   ] .

Add-on
Find out how porcupines are different from hedgehogs,
using a reference book.

New words

Change the ending sound of each word to make a new word.
You can use:

g   k   p   r   v   x   z

One word can't be changed with any of these letters.

The word that can't be changed is:

boot	boo __	wake	wa __ e
quit	qui __	fire	fi __ e
stove	sto __ e	time	ti __ e
side	si __ e	wag	wa __
sheet	shee __	ride	ri __ e
bat	ba __	flap	fla __
snip	sni __	plum	plu __

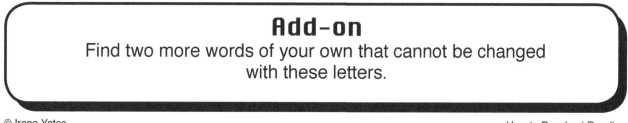

Add-on
Find two more words of your own that cannot be changed
with these letters.

Add letters

Add one letter to make words. The first one has been done for you.

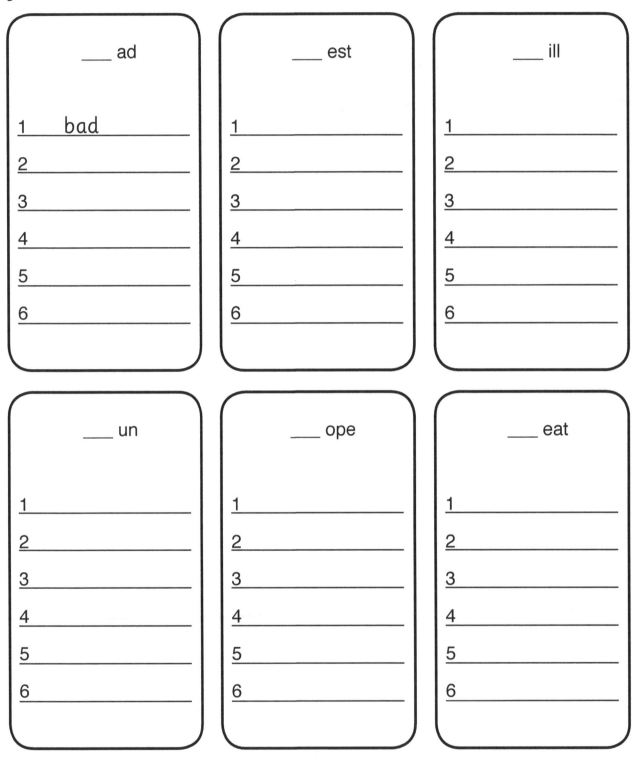

___ ad

1 bad
2
3
4
5
6

___ est

1
2
3
4
5
6

___ ill

1
2
3
4
5
6

___ un

1
2
3
4
5
6

___ ope

1
2
3
4
5
6

___ eat

1
2
3
4
5
6

Add-on
Can you add *two* letters to any of the sounds to make new words?

Making words

Add letters to make words. One of each has already been done for you.

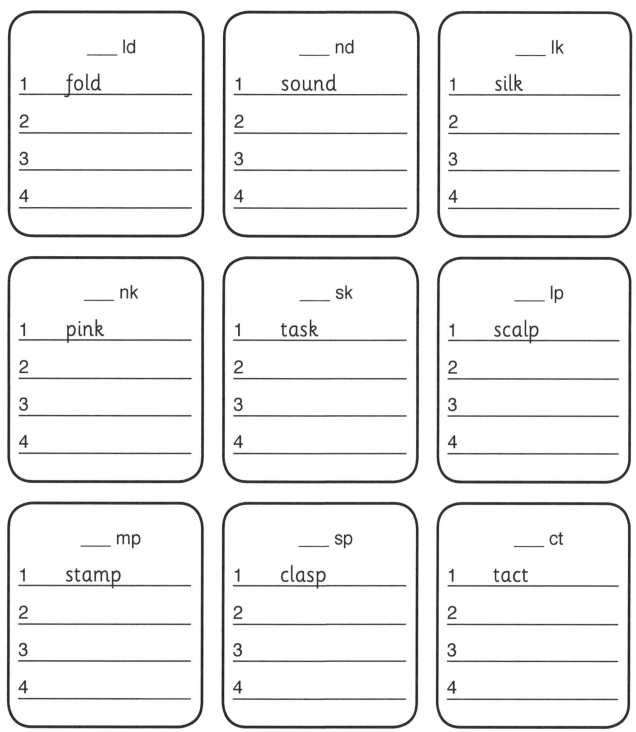

___ ld
1   fold
2   _____
3   _____
4   _____

___ nd
1   sound
2   _____
3   _____
4   _____

___ lk
1   silk
2   _____
3   _____
4   _____

___ nk
1   pink
2   _____
3   _____
4   _____

___ sk
1   task
2   _____
3   _____
4   _____

___ lp
1   scalp
2   _____
3   _____
4   _____

___ mp
1   stamp
2   _____
3   _____
4   _____

___ sp
1   clasp
2   _____
3   _____
4   _____

___ ct
1   tact
2   _____
3   _____
4   _____

Add-on
Check your words in a dictionary.

Making more words

Add letters to make words. One of each has already been done for you.

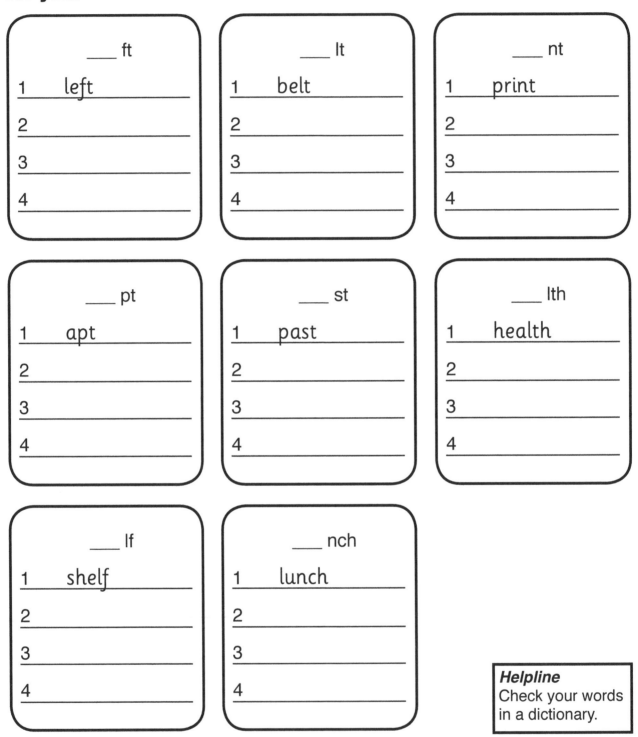

___ ft
1   left
2   ____
3   ____
4   ____

___ lt
1   belt
2   ____
3   ____
4   ____

___ nt
1   print
2   ____
3   ____
4   ____

___ pt
1   apt
2   ____
3   ____
4   ____

___ st
1   past
2   ____
3   ____
4   ____

___ lth
1   health
2   ____
3   ____
4   ____

___ lf
1   shelf
2   ____
3   ____
4   ____

___ nch
1   lunch
2   ____
3   ____
4   ____

Helpline
Check your words in a dictionary.

Add-on
Find two words ending with 'xt'.

Which shape?

Read the words carefully.

If a word has a short vowel sound, draw a red circle round it.

If it has a long vowel sound, draw a green box round it.

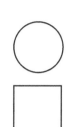

miss   act   fade   mind

bad

know   grain

junk

crisp

gold   craze

grip

bed

fame

jade

fight

gong   crime

sigh

golf

knock   kind

bead

Add-on
Write six new words with short vowels,
and six new words with long vowels.

Double-up

Compound words are made up of two smaller words. For example:

milkshake   =   milk   +   shake

Your task is to split each compound word into its two parts.

milkman = [　　　　] + [　　　　]

cupboard = [　　　　] + [　　　　]

himself = [　　　　] + [　　　　]

handbag = [　　　　] + [　　　　]

teaspoon = [　　　　] + [　　　　]

butterfly = [　　　　] + [　　　　]

airport = [　　　　] + [　　　　]

clockwork = [　　　　] + [　　　　]

homesick = [　　　　] + [　　　　]

bulldoze = [　　　　] + [　　　　]

featherweight = [　　　　] + [　　　　]

firefighter = [　　　　] + [　　　　]

Add-on
Use a dictionary to find six more compound words.

Words within words

Sometimes you can see another word inside a word. All of the words on this page have smaller words inside them.

Your task is to find the small words. Underline the words and write them in the box. The first one has been done for you.

ab<u>out</u>

out

abrupt

actor

bonnet

brother

candle

capable

cassette

covered

formal

for<u>got</u>ten

Helpline
You may be able to find more than one word inside some words! If you do, write all the words you find.

Add-on
Choose four of the small words you have found,
and write a sentence for each.

Words inside words

Sometimes you can see another word inside a word. All of the words on this page have smaller words inside them.

Your task is to find the small words. Underline the words and write them in the box. The first one has been done for you.

li<u>on</u>

on

luggage

market

measure

mongoose

narrow

novel

observer

outlandish

parachute

parsnip

Helpline
You may be able to find more than one word inside some words! If you do, write all the words you find.

Add-on
Choose four of the small words you have found,
and write a sentence for each.

Learn to scan

These words are all in the following piece of information.

break	pulled	meat	whole	bones
needles	prey	animals	rest	leopard

Read the piece carefully. Look for the words and mark them with a highlighter pen. Time yourself to see how long it takes.

What do snakes eat?

All snakes eat meat of some kind. They eat their meals whole, without chewing them. Snakes' teeth cannot break or cut up food. Their teeth are like needles. They are used to pull the prey into the snake's mouth.

A snake's jaws are attached very loosely to the other bones of its skull. Snakes eat by pushing one jaw bone over the food while the teeth of the rest of the jaw hold the meat. Then another jaw bone pushes over the food and it is pulled down the snake's throat.

Snakes can eat all kinds of animals; a python can even eat a leopard or a deer!

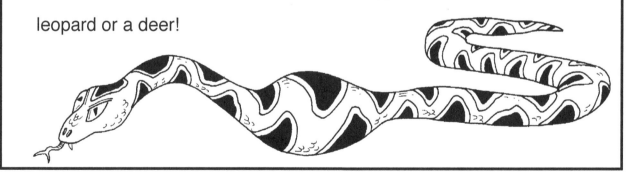

It took me _____ minutes to find the ten words.

Add-on
Tell a friend how snakes eat.

Scanning to read

These words are all in the following piece of information.

down   people   move   clouds   direction

meteors   zigzag   travel   doughnuts   speeds

Read the piece carefully. Look for the words and mark them with a highlighter pen. Time yourself to see how long it takes.

What are UFOs?

UFO stands for Unidentified Flying Object. Sometimes people call them flying saucers. Lots of people think they have seen flying saucers.

Some people have seen flat saucers, some sphere-shaped saucers, some UFOs shaped like cigars or doughnuts. Saucers have been seen to moving in every direction and at all speeds. Some hang in the air. Some move straight up or down. Some travel in a zigzag.

Scientists think that most of the things seen are not UFOs at all. They are satellites or clouds or meteors. Some might be birds or planets or fireworks. They might even be fireballs, formed by lightning.

It took me _____ minutes to find the ten words.

Add-on
Tell a friend what UFOs are.